SINEWS OF FAITH

SINEWS OF FAITH

BY

DONALD COGGAN
ARCHBISHOP OF YORK

A Primary Visitation Charge
to the Diocese of York
April 1969

HODDER AND STOUGHTON

DEDICATED TO
the clergy and laity
of the Diocese of York
for whom and with whom
it is my privilege to
work in the service of
our common Lord

May God's Spirit enlighten your mind and soul. May His love fill your heart and keep you equally from pride and despair, and may His good hand lead you kindly upon your path to His glory and to the blessing of all you have to take care of. And may the blessing of God the Father, the Son and the Holy Spirit, be amongst you and remain with you always.

Man has now decisively overcome Nature by his technology; but the victor has been technology, not Man himself. Man has merely exchanged one master for another, and his new master is more overbearing than his former one. Man is still the slave of his environment.

Arnold Toynbee, Experiences, p. 326

O Lord our God, let us hope in the protecting shadow of Thy wings. Guard us and bear us up. Bear us up Thou wilt, as tiny infants and on to our grey hairs: for when Thou art our strength, it is strength indeed, but when our strength is our own it is only weakness.

Augustine, Confessions, IV, xvi

PREFACE

THE addresses in this little book were given as my Primary Visitation Charge in the Diocese of York. The first was delivered in the Cathedral and Metropolitical Church of St. Peter, York, the second in Selby Abbey, the third in Holy Trinity, Hull, the fourth in Bridlington Priory, the fifth in St. John's, Middlesbrough, and the sixth in the Parish Church of Pickering.

The congregations consisted of the clergy of the diocese, the Readers, the Women Workers, the Church Army captains and sisters, the Archbishop's Messengers, the Church Wardens, and two members from every parochial church council. There were also present the Suffragan Bishops and Archdeacons, the Chancellor of the Diocese (Dr. W. S. Wigglesworth), the Registrar (Mr. G. P. Knowles), and my chaplains (the Rev. A. M. A. Turnbull and Mr. D. A. C. Blunt) to whom I owe so much.

Each address was delivered in the context of a service of worship; I have given, under the title of the address, the references of the passage or passages of Scripture which were read in the service.

The audience largely provided me with the subjects on which I felt I must speak. That is to say, I saw these occasions as opportunities to share with my fellow-workers in Christ some of my concerns for the diocese of which we all were representatives, though I had in view also the Province of which the diocese is a part and the Church beyond its bounds. The addresses are the result of journeys up and down the diocese over a period of more than eight years, following on my work as Bishop of Bradford for five and a half. I have tried to put my finger on the things to which I believe we must address ourselves in the years of the new decade soon to open before us – things which, if neglected, will lead to slumber and death, but, if put first in thought and action, will lead to new life in and through the Body of Christ.

It is my prayer that, as these pages are read and pondered, they may cause some to lay hold more firmly than ever on the things which cannot be shaken and may bring assurance to those whose footsteps have well-nigh slipped.

Bishopthorpe York

DONALD EBOR:

CONTENTS

I

'THE GIFT OF TRUE DISCRIMINATION'
(Philippians i, 3–21)

THERE is an old Latin tag which runs: *Corruptio optimi pessima*, which being roughly translated means: the best things gone wrong are very bad indeed. This is true in everyday life. The higher your view, say, of sex, the worse does its prostitution seem to you; the greater the honour you accord to marriage, the greater your sorrow at divorce. And so on. No less is this true in the realm of Christian thinking, of theology and ethics. The history of Christian thought is strewn with the tragedies of a good doctrine or idea so twisted, or so narrowed, as to be radically distorted and therefore dangerous. I wish to speak of certain such areas of thought at present current among us.

I

I believe that one of the most encouraging signs of this generation, and perhaps especially of its younger members, is its strong social concern. When I hear of young people being somewhat sweepingly condemned and their spirit of rebellion being castigated, I point to the lively social conscience which often animates them. Student revolt is often ill-expressed; but again and again it takes the form it does because those who engage in it can find no better way of expressing their disgust at iniquities to which some of us older people have grown all too easily accustomed. The form of rebellion may be like that of a tiger trying to claw its way out of a net in which it is entangled – it is savage and 'unorganised'. But at least it is not acquiescent, which is more than can be said of many whose youthful fires of rebellion have been damped down by the comforts of middle age and after. I fully recognise that student revolt is sometimes fomented by influences which are sinister and sometimes wholly bad. But in many cases the real thing is there. They want to say – and say loudly and clearly – that they will not stand for inequalities of opportunity, for racism, for Rachmanism, for war. At its best, such youthful rebellion takes the positive shape of service in Voluntary Service Overseas or in community service at home. More power to those who engage in such work!

In Christian theology, this emphasis can be seen in the stress which has recently been laid, and is still being laid, by a galaxy of writers on Christ as the Servant, on the Church as the Servant Church, and on the individual Christian as being himself the servant of Christ, and of others for Christ's sake. This is wholly good and is much to be welcomed, provided that the distinction is clearly observed between service and servitude, between service and servility. A recent editorial in *Theology* (December, 1968) uttered a warning about such a confusion and a protest against excessive breast-beating, hand-wringing, and obsessive guilt feelings on the part of the leaders of the Church. It criticised the Lambeth Conference Report for reflecting 'the paradox of the present mood, in which preoccupation with the miseries of the world and anxiety for the Church to serve it result in the too ready acceptance of prescriptions which will reduce the Church to such servitude ... that it becomes incapable of serving the world, and doubtful of its own intrinsic worth'. The point is well made and well taken.

To revert to the idea of the Servant (Christ, Church, individual). In missionary work abroad, any hint of paternalistic benevolence immediately meets with resentment. The sensitive modern missionary eschews any suggestion that the whiteness of his skin justifies any element of domination in approach to those among whom he works. It may be historically true that the great missionary movement of the Church, say from A.D. 1800, followed in the wake of the growth of the British Empire. But any touch of 'imperialism' now only invites a response of resentment, and may easily lead to extradition of the missionary by the local government authorities. The chief offices of the Church, in Africa, Asia, and elsewhere, are increasingly held by nationals, with the white man occupying the 'inferior' posts in those countries where he is allowed to remain. This is not to be resented. It is to be accepted, even welcomed. 'The Son of Man did not come to be served but to serve ...' (St. Mark x, 45).

Because the Christian is in the world, because he is a follower of the Incarnate Lord, he must be deeply concerned with 'the miseries of this sinful world'. He must never contract out into an 'other-worldliness' which would relieve him of participation in effort for social amelioration, or which would free him from the hard intellectual discipline of wrestling either with the problems created by a welfare state or with the problems of countries which lack such a system. Any theology which is not grounded in an incarnational theology may be expected to produce the kind of disastrous results which follow from any theological imbalance.

In a memorable speech made at the Fourth Assembly of the World Council of Churches at Uppsala in July 1968, the British representative at the United Nations, Lord Caradon, said this: 'There is ... a growing apathy in many Western nations towards world affairs. The apathy turns to antipathy. There is a creeping indifference and an ingrowing irritation ... There is a turning away in bewilderment and suburban selfishness, or in what U Thant calls prosperous provincialism, from the bad news coming from Asia and Africa' (Kenneth Slack, *Uppsala Report*, p. 33, S.C.M. Press). It is an ill day for the Church when that spirit invades it. Was the speaker who preceded Lord Caradon, the Negro novelist James Baldwin, wholly wrong when he began his address by saying: 'I address you as one of the creatures, one of God's creatures, whom the Christian Church has most betrayed,' and when he ended it with these words: 'When a structure, no matter what structure it may be, a state or a church or a country, becomes too expensive for the world to afford, when it is no longer responsive to the needs of the world, that structure, sooner or later – and quite apart from the will of any man – is doomed. If the Christian faith does not recover its Lord and Saviour Jesus Christ, then we will discover the meaning of what he meant when he said, "Insofar as you have not done it unto the least of those, you have not done it unto me" '? (Kenneth Slack, *op. cit.*, pp. 31–33).

I have, I think, said enough to make it clear I hold that any Christian who has not got a social conscience is a very poor Christian, if indeed he can be called a Christian at all. The thinking Christian must attach immense importance to the study of sociology, and that on a world scale, *the while he makes it clear that he is far more than a sociologist*. And it is precisely here that so often the distortion is to be found.

Social concern is not the Gospel, though it is part of the Gospel. Looking back over the two great Christian Conferences of the summer of 1968, the World Council of Churches at Uppsala and the Lambeth Conference, one is conscious of and profoundly thankful for the sensitiveness to social wrongs which animated the speeches, and the concern for necessary change in the Church and in the Christian. But as one reviews the Conferences and reads the Reports, one is constrained to ask whether Bishop George Bell's criticism of the 1958 Lambeth Conference might not also be made of these two: 'Too little of supernatural or spiritual or (if preferred) too little of the theological approach anywhere.' Kenneth Slack in his *Uppsala Report* writes:

'I wondered whether the demonic power of evil was being seen sufficiently clearly – that power that struck down Martin Luther King, our preacher, and that held Nigerian and Biafran in its grip, refusing to allow the invasion of reconciling love. Was the power of evil to divide the "human" – a word that

17

rang through Uppsala – sufficiently stressed, and with it God's answer? Were the Cross and Resurrection central enough?' (p. 88).

Even more damningly, a reviewer of the *Lambeth Conference Report* wrote: 'I believe that the Report, as it stands, tends to produce the impression that the Church as a whole is justified by its social and economic service.' Dr. Olivier Béguin wrote:

'The sensitivity to the changes in the world and the concern for parallel necessary changes in the Church and Christian approach to the world have resulted in an unhappy near oversight of the basic sinfulness of man and his need for forgiveness and redemption. It often looks as though this new humanity (a term much debated in certain sections) were to be achieved simply by Christian presence in the world as almost the only form of witness to Jesus Christ . . .' (United Bible Societies *Bulletin*, No. 76, p. 178).

This distortion is present not only in the great conferences of the Church. It seeps, like some chilly fog, into the pulpits of our land. At its worst, it takes the form of a hesitancy in speaking about God, about Christ, about the energy of the Holy Spirit, about sin and redemption. It issues in a dethronement of Christ from the central place which is His by right.

The oft-quoted, popular passage which begins 'The Son of Man did not come to be served but to serve' does not end there. It goes on, *'and to surrender his life as a ransom for many'* (St. Mark x, 45). Jesus is not only the Servant; He is also the Redeemer from sin. His ministry impinges very closely on man's social welfare, his health of body and mind. But it goes deeper, right down to man's radical wrongness, treating his 'Fall' with all possible seriousness and providing a remedy for it which man by himself cannot provide. There can be little doubt that 'the fundamental ideas' of this 'ransom' saying 'are those of Isaiah 53' (Vincent Taylor: *Jesus and His Sacrifice*, p. 105), and that is highly significant.

Almost as popular in recent writing as the idea of the servant Christ, has been the idea of 'the man for others'. Jesus was supremely 'the Man for others', and so should His followers be. But the phrase needs further definition. What is meant by *'for'* when used with reference to our Lord? I do not think that this question can be answered until we have determined what Jesus meant when He thought of Himself as the Servant of the Lord. I believe that he had meditated long and deeply on the four Servant Songs of Isaiah which culminate in chapter fifty-three. What is the picture there given? Mysterious as it is in many of its parts, certain features are luminously clear. One is that the Servant is far more than a great humanitarian endowed with an alert social conscience. He is 'the man for others' precisely because he is the man *with God's word for others*. The Jerusalem Bible rendering of Isaiah 1, 4 makes this clear: 'The Lord Yahweh has given me a disciple's tongue. So that I may know how to reply to the wearied he provides me with speech. Each morning he wakes me to hear, to listen like a disciple. The Lord Yahweh has opened my ear.' Here we see a man provided by the Lord with a word to speak – a word the delivery of which was to prove unpopular and costly (Isaiah 1, 6–7, and chapter liii). He is the servant of the Lord not in the sense that he is a humanitarian, great and good as that office undoubtedly is, but in the sense that he is the guardian, the deliverer, the exponent of certain truths without which man cannot be whole. For, as Jesus was to say at the beginning of His ministry: 'Man cannot live on bread alone; he lives on every word that God utters' (St. Matthew iv, 4).

A concern for this world, its glories, its miseries, its potentialities, is wholly right. It is God's world – by creation (Genesis i and ii) and by redemption (St. John iii, 16 *et al.*). But it also 'lies in the power of the evil one' (1 St. John v, 19) and is in need of radical redemption. It is marked by transitoriness (1 St. John ii, 17). Here, precisely, is the point of tension for the Christian. He must have commerce constantly with the ephemeral, transitory world-order; in it he is to be 'the man for others', seeking to bring the mind of God to bear on its problems, its inequities and its iniquities. But he must range out beyond *this* world into *that*. Only in so far as he does that will his ministry be faithful to the Son of Man who served and redeemed. 'There is a mentality so insulated within its own secular frontiers as not to be concerned either with the past or with eternity' – so writes the Archbishop of Canterbury of a phase in our culture which lacks affection for past tradition and concern for a world beyond this (A. M. Ramsay, *God, Christ and the World*, p. 15, S.C.M. Press). God's men do well to be on the watch against infection by such a spirit. I well recall hearing Bishop C. S. Woodward, then Bishop of Bristol, asking a conference of men concerned with the training of ordinands: 'Are we teaching our people *how to die*?'

The Christian Gospel spans both worlds, links time and eternity. While we moderns have done absolutely rightly in throwing overboard a theology which so stresses the future as to minimise the importance of the present, we have no right to go to the other extreme and fail to speak a clear word about that future life towards which we all inexorably move.

II

I have spoken at such length about this particular 'distortion' that I must be much briefer about certain others which give me to think.

Ecumenism, church unity, is in the air. It is *the* theme in Church circles – and indeed beyond. Constantly on my journeys this is the subject on which reporters wish to question me – re-union with Rome, with the Methodists, and so on. This has caught the imagination both of the Church and of the world. And that is good. After all, there is still something of novelty about ecumenism – if Edinburgh 1910 be thought of as the beginning of what we know as the ecumenical movement, that is less than sixty years ago. Historically it is hardly correct to think of that great Conference as the beginning of ecumenism, for the movement had been prepared for by the friendships and co-operation offered by joint work in such movements as the Young Men's (and Young Women's) Christian Association and in the Bible Societies. But Edinburgh 1910 was the first of that great series of World Conferences which gave birth to the 'Life and Work' and 'Faith and Order' movements, then to the World Council of Churches, and so has culminated in the Third Assembly at New Delhi (when the Orthodox were admitted) and the Fourth Assembly at Uppsala 1968, when 232 churches were represented, and 800 official delegates and a total of some 2,000 people were present.

As we review the story during this twentieth century, how much we have to thank God for! The steady growth of a desire for Church unity; the mounting volume of prayer for it; the love and understanding which have been taking the place of suspicion often based on ignorance of one another's ways; joint work and, often, joint worship – all this is cause for thanksgiving. We must not let up. We must press the advantages that love and new knowledge have gained over the forces of divisiveness. We must not rest till the scandal of disunity ceases – a disunity which can keep separate at the Lord's Table those who have been united in the same Lord's sacrament of baptism. Timidity and fear of the unknown must not be allowed to inhibit further progress towards union.

But ecumenism *can* become a kind of hobby. I am not referring only to those so-called 'ecumaniacs' who 'spend their time in nothing else but either to tell or to hear some new thing' at some new conference which debates ecumenicity! I am thinking of a subtle temptation which comes to a much bigger company of Christians – the temptation to be so absorbed in the *good* of unity that they forget the *best* which is the purpose of the search for it, viz. 'that the world may believe' (St. John xvii, 21). If half the passion which is to-day being manifested in the search for unity, in the cultivating of ecumenicity, were spent on the pursuit for Christ's sake of those who know Him not, the picture of the Church would be a far healthier one than it now is and the world itself would be a saner and a safer place. All too easily local ecumenical discussion groups can degenerate into *merely* discussion groups, with no evangelistic outcome and no impact on the world around. If it is true, as I believe it is, that truth is found *on the road* and not on some philosophical balcony remote from life, so I believe it is equally true that unity is found *on the road*. Joint evangelistic endeavour must go hand in hand with ecumenical discussion. Otherwise a radical distortion will set in, in our efforts towards unity.

III

A further area in which distortion can easily take place is the area of our Church life which can be described by the word stewardship. It has been defined as 'an attitude of one's mind and life. Stewardship essentially is realising that everything I am and have comes from God and that I must be answerable to Him for the use I make of what He has lent me.' The writer goes on to say that for many years he has tried to give away at least one tenth of everything that has come to him in the way of income or gifts and has never found this burdensome or difficult. 'It seems to me a very natural acknowledgement of the astonishing goodness and grace of God to me.' With this as the fundamental meaning of stewardship I would fully agree – it enshrines a Biblical and thoroughly Christian approach to life, talents, and property.

But how easily can this principle be twisted, distorted, misrepresented. Too many regard stewardship as *primarily* being concerned with money. Some even think of it as almost exclusively a fund-raising movement – 'Our Church finances are in a bad way, the Church or Hall needs redecorating or the boiler renewing; *so* let us have a stewardship campaign.' Thus, a movement which concerns the whole of life and of Christian discipleship is reduced to become a movement concerned with a part (albeit an important part) of life, the financial. It is this narrowing of the horizons which constitutes a distortion of a very noble idea.

We began with the Latin tag: *Corruptio optimi pessima*. We end on a more positive note – the prayer of St. Paul for his friends at Philippi: 'This is my prayer, that your love may grow ever richer and richer in knowledge and insight of every kind, and may thus bring you the gift of true discrimination' (Philippians i, 9–10). Love – knowledge – insight – discrimination. It is a goodly quartet and one greatly to be coveted and prayed for.

2

'I WANT YOU'

(Psalm lxiii, 1–8; 1 Thessalonians v, 14–24)

WHEN I was more than half-way through the preparation
of the addresses which I am giving in the six centres
where this Primary Visitation is being held, I jotted
down on a scrap of paper the words: 'Dare I do one
on Prayer?' There were various factors which made
me pose the question in that form. For one thing, I am
all too conscious that I am not very good at prayer
myself – no graduate here, only a preparatory school
boy. For another, so much has been written on the subject already, that he who speaks about it runs the risk
of plagiarism or boredom. For another, I had said a
good deal of what is uppermost in my mind on this
matter in a book published in 1967 – *The Prayers of
the New Testament*. There, in a sense, it was com-
paratively easy to write on this subject, for the 'bones'
were there already; one had only to work through the
books of the New Testament, dig out the prayers, look
them in the face, and comment on them with what
measure of scholarship and insight one might be able
to summon up.

But, for all my hesitations, the subject nagged at me;
perhaps 'challenged me' would be a better way of expressing it. The audience which I was to address
would be a specialist one – the clergy of the diocese,

the Readers, the Women Workers, the Church Army officers, Archbishop's Messengers, Church Wardens, and members of parochial church councils – in fact, every one of them men and women in positions of responsibility and leadership in our diocese. Every one of those who would be listening to me would be a learner in the school of prayer, and every one should be a teacher of others in that same school, whether he taught formally from the pulpit or informally in conversation, sharing with others what he was finding to be true and discussing it with them in the give and take of natural conversation. That consideration alone provided sufficient justification for an attempt to say something about prayer in our own experience and about the teaching of prayer to our contemporaries. This, then, had to be my theme.

I

Prayer in our own experience. I begin with a quotation from an article in *The Times* of last February 22nd. 'Much of the present fretfulness among both ordained and lay Christians, and the general lack of large-mindedness in our ecclesiastical affairs, is due to a defect resembling physical under-nourishment: a stunted capacity to stretch and grow in learning, in prayer, and in spiritual perspective.' The writer shows a keen capacity for diagnosis of our ills. 'Fretfulness' – how right he is in fastening on this as characteristic of many Christians to-day! Because the Christian way is not popular, because people do not (generally speaking) flock to Church, because the winds are contrary, we fret, and the joy of God is conspicuous by its absence from our faces. 'Lack of large-mindedness in our ecclesiastical affairs' – how often we see this manifested in the way, for example, that we face, so fearfully, Anglican–Methodist union, or in the way we succumb to a narrow parochialism, when the *world* is our parish just because Christ died for it! The writer attributed this malaise to a stunted growth in learning, in prayer, and in spiritual perspective. Stunted growth in prayer – it is all too true. There are Christian men and women in their thirties, forties, fifties who have not got far beyond the prayer: 'Gentle Jesus, meek and mild, look upon a little child', or beyond the *pattering* of the Lord's Prayer. There are clergy who, having hurried through the Offices of the day, think that their work of prayer is done; there are other clergy who have abandoned the Offices and – quite apart from the rightness or wrongness of this – have found no adequate substitute for them. There are some who would very much resent any suggestion that they are not Christians, who indeed occupy positions of responsibility in the Christian community, who have, for all intents and purposes, given up prayer except on Sundays when they go to church. And when they get there, they find themselves singing: 'We perish if we cease from prayer.' What is this hymn-writer saying – is he giving way to wild poetic license? Or is this down-right spiritual, factual common-sense, a reference to the stunting of growth which our writer in *The Times* spoke of? The sort of thing that happens in your garden, when you put in a good, healthy plant, and forget to feed it and water it?

I suspect that here we are on to something of immense importance – far more important than new forms of Church government, new 'structures', new canons, new services, new fund-raising schemes, or even plans for Church unity; more important than these because all of these things, and a hundred others besides, will be radically affected by what we think about prayer and what we do about it. *This* is basic. The other things are consequential. Get *this* wrong, and the stunting process sets in, the fretfulness, the lack of large-mindedness in ecclesiastical (and other) affairs. Get *this* right, and the odds are that there will be growth, a certain serenity and joy which come from getting one's perspectives right, a certain large-mindedness and large-heartedness which can only come from companying with God.

Now this may give us a clue to the meaning of prayer. If you love somebody, you want to be with them – that is a fact of human experience which every happily married couple knows, and which becomes truer to them as the decades go by. It is true also, though I suspect in a lesser degree, of many other kinds of friendship. You want to be with them – your companionship may issue in words, or it may take place in complete silence. That matters little. You are in the presence of the other, and that is enough. 'I love you. I want you' – these deep feelings are satisfied by the one being in the presence of the other.

Father Robert Mercer, of the Community of the Resurrection, wrote an article in a recent issue of the Community's *Quarterly Review* (No. 263) entitled: 'Is Prayer Any Use?' It began: 'No, it's not. Those of you who know Bob Dylan's record "I Want You", need no lecture on prayer. Over and over again he sings, "*I want you, I want you. I want you*", and although his record is about a boy and a girl, he is giving a vivid description of prayer.' Father Mercer ended his article thus: 'Is prayer any use? No, it's not. Effects, yes. Uses, none. Do you use those you love . . .? If so, that's selfishness, not love. The Church does not make use of God for some purpose outside of or apart from Himself. We desire Him for His own sake. "Thou, O God, hast made us for Thyself and our heart knows no rest until it rests in Thee." '

The Psalmists knew a great deal about this. 'My soul is athirst for God, yea, even for the living God.' 'I will love Thee, O Lord, my strength' – and so on. But there, just there, is our trouble. They were giants, so it would seem. We are puny. We *don't* feel thirsty, or loving God-wards. This should not trouble us over-much – feelings are poor things to judge by. The fact that we are concerned about prayer at all is quite enough to go on. It is a spark that could be fanned into a flame. And after all, prayer, like any other kind of spiritual activity, is only a response to the God who was always there, busy long before we showed a glimmer of interest.

I sought the Lord, and afterward I knew
He moved my soul to seek him, seeking me;
It was not that I found, O Saviour true,
But I was found of thee.

Thou didst reach forth thy hand, and mine enfold;
I walked, and sank not, in the storm-vexed sea;
'Twas not so much that I on thee took hold,
As thou, dear Lord, on me.

I followed, loved: but of my love, the whole
Is but my answer, Lord of love, to thee;
For thou wast long beforehand with my soul:
Always thou lovedst me.

Just before Christmas last year there was a Leader on
Prayer in *The Times*. It was written by – guess whom.
Not a well-known religious, or retreat-conductor, but
by Cecil King, newspaper magnate; and a great deal of
good sense there was in it. It was headed: 'Prayer as
an act of listening, not asking', and it included the
sentence: 'To me prayer is listening, not asking.' Perhaps that is an over-simplification, for I suspect that
the Father likes the child to ask Him for things, even
though the Father knows our needs before we ask, and
even though the child has got well beyond asking for
a bicycle or for a change in the weather to suit his particular desires for a garden-party! But Cecil King was
on to a point of importance – 'prayer is listening', he
said, and he went on to say that 'as the voice may be
faint and the message both unexpected and unwel-
come, it takes much practice and much patience'.
Browning, you may remember, spoke about 'God
whispering us in the ear'. But what does this amount
to *in practice*? I suspect that it leads us straight – and
inexorably – into some kind of spiritual discipline,
some kind of planned 'going aside from the multitude'.
Let me say at once that for different people this will
mean very different things. It will mean one thing to
the parish priest who, rising early, gets a regular hour
in his church before going home to his breakfast,
lovingly prepared by his wife. It will mean quite an-

other thing for the mother who has five children all waiting to be fed and got off to school! But whether it means a regular hour in the morning, or five minutes snatched after lunch, or ten minutes before bed at night, some kind of discipline is, I believe, called for if we are to hear 'God whispering us in the ear', if we are to escape stunted growth.

Now this, to many, will be a glimpse of the obvious. But I think it needs saying especially to-day. There are those who would abandon any such regularised, set-aside periods, any such almost regimented discipline as I have envisaged. *Laborare est orare*, they would say – do your job for Christ's sake, and you have done your praying. That sounds good – and *is* good, so far as it goes. We must learn to pray on a bus or in the train. We must learn to pray walking along the road. We must learn to shoot up a prayer before knocking on a door or answering a letter or beginning an interview. And the visit or the letter or the interview carried out in the name and for the sake of Christ is in a sense a prayer offered to God. Let that be granted – and gladly. But I do not believe that that will do – just like that; not if we are to grow, with roots healthily downwards and fruit abundantly upward. This *by itself* lays us open to all the perils of activism, which one of our own clergy has described as one of the main diseases in the Church to-day. By activism I mean the refusal to stop, to think, to read, to listen, to resolve; the confusion of the perspiration of activity with the inspiration of God.

Much is heard to-day of 'religionless Christianity'. The phrase was one used often by Dietrich Bonhoeffer, even if it did not owe its origin to him. To many who use it somewhat cavalierly it means the throwing over not only of set forms of service but also those disciplines of the spiritual life which, in one form or another, have marked the Church all down the ages. But let us be careful here. Eberhard Bethge, who was Bonhoeffer's closest friend and who has become his definitive biographer, has said: 'The isolated use and handing down of the famous term "religionless Christianity" has made Bonhoeffer the champion of an undialectical shallow modernism which obscures all that he wanted to tell us about the living God' (quoted in Mary Bosanquet, *The Life and Death of Dietrich Bonhoeffer*, p. 279). To quote Bethge again: 'Secret discipline without worldliness becomes pure ghetto; worldliness without the secret discipline pure boulevard.' Now Bonhoeffer escaped the perils both of ghetto and of boulevard, of withdrawal from the world into an 'other-worldliness' which is un-Christlike, and of involvement in the world ('boulevard-ism') which neglects withdrawal for thought, communion with God, prayer. Let us never talk about 'religionless Christianity' with a kind of nod of acknowledgement to Bonhoeffer until we have read his Life. If ever there was a man who learnt and practised the discipline of daily withdrawal, who worked at his prayer life, it was Bonhoeffer. Listen to this: 'Our relationship with God must be practised, otherwise we shall not find the right note, the right word, the right language when He comes upon us unawares. We have to learn the language of God, learn it with effort, we must work at it, if we too would learn to converse with Him; prayer too

must be practised as part of our work' (*op. cit.*, p. 70).
An indispensable part of this daily withdrawal was,
for Bonhoeffer, the slow reading of the Bible. In a
letter to a friend he wrote: 'I read [the Bible] in the
morning and the evening, often during the day as well,
and every day I consider a text which I have chosen
for the whole week, and try to sink deeply into it, so
as really to hear what it is saying. I know that without
this I could not live properly any longer. And I certainly could not believe ...' (*op. cit.*, p. 110). 'This
steady attempt to follow Jesus,' says Mary Bosanquet
of Bonhoeffer, 'was supported by the inspiration of the
daily reading and prayer which was now a discipline
never omitted, and whose power was penetrating ever
deeper into the hidden roots of his life, to issue more
and more frequently as the years went by in the direct
and powerful insights which so often set him apart
from those who were not capable of this kind of perception' (*op. cit.*, p. 148). Enough said – prayer as the
road to perception; prayer as the answer to stunted
growth and to fretfulness and to lack of large-mindedness; prayer as the way to share God's perspectives
and thus to avoid, *inter alia,* the depression which
comes from missing the wood for the trees.

I must add here a word, which has a particular bear-
ing for the clergy, about the use of the Daily Offices. I
am aware of a restlessness about the regular use of these
Offices on the part of some of the clergy, perhaps par-
ticularly of the younger ones. I understand this, for I
am one who only came to appreciate their value after
some years in the ministry. I am grateful for the work
which the Joint Liturgical Group has done in pioneer-

ing a little book entitled *The Daily Office* (S.P.C.K. and Epworth Press, 1969, 12*s*. 6*d*.), which puts forward suggestions for a Daily Office which is shorter and more varied than our present one and which, while embodying traditional elements familiar to Anglicans, seeks to meet a need felt by a significant number of Free Church ministers. There is ample room for experiment and enrichment and I am not one of those who simply want a continuation of the *status quo*. The point I want to make here, however, is this: for most of us, if not for all, some kind of regular, structural guidance is necessary, some kind of liturgical scaffolding, some defined diet of reading and prayer, of penitence and thanksgiving. Otherwise, we so easily and so soon become the victims of our own feelings, yielding to our little devotional whims, dependent on the state of our physical or psychological health – and this, if continued over the years, can lead to spiritual anaemia. We should avail ourselves of the wisdom and the support of the *Church*.

If, as I believe and as I have tried to point out, we need a structure for our daily worship, we also need a plan for our daily intercession. Here some care is called for. The parish priest may well decide to pray for a different street of his parish each day, mentally walking down that street and bringing those known to him, and those unknown, before God. I hope that every parish in this diocese, if it does not already do so, will use our diocesan cycle of prayer so that, on any given day, the whole diocesan family is united in prayer for the clergy and people of a particular parish. I can conceive of no greater bond of unity and strength than this. And the Anglican cycle of prayer – the constant use of this will save us from becoming parochially minded in our praying. The wise use of this cycle will enable our people to 'lift up their eyes and look on the fields'. Incidentally, when this becomes pivotal in our parochial praying, it is likely that many parishes will find that ten per cent as a minimum for giving outside the parish concerned is inadequate. Prayer and sacrificial giving have a way of going together.

II

What am I to say about *the teaching of prayer to our contemporaries?* I can say but little, and that largely along the lines of a few practical suggestions. I note that it was the sight of Jesus at prayer that made one of His disciples say, 'Lord, teach us to pray' (St. Luke xi, 1) – which gives me the hint that the best way I can teach others to pray is to get on with it myself! When people see a man of prayer among them, their appetite for prayer is often whetted.

Those who are responsible for the conduct of public worship can do much. I am speaking elsewhere in these addresses about the use of silence in public worship, surely an essential ingredient, but how often does one find it lacking! (p. 42–5). I take for granted the saying of prayers at a rate which is reverent and in a voice which makes the participation of the laity easy. I would plead for a rearrangement of order in Mattins and Evensong which I find all too rare as I go about, namely, the putting of 'the prayers after the third collect' *not* directly after the third collect! They come far better after the sermon – the order thus being:

third collect, (notices), hymn, sermon, prayers. These prayers, carefully prepared to fit in with the theme of the sermon, can well serve to clinch its message and are far more effective than a (sometimes hurried and often formal) Ascription.

It has been said that many Christians are like the River St. Lawrence in winter time – frozen at the mouth! That is all too true; and it comes as something of a release when the oft-repeated prayer 'O Lord, open Thou our lips' is literally answered and the lay member of the Church ventures to pray aloud. There are many ways to help him. I note the growing habit of saying 'The Grace' congregationally; this can be extended to other prayers, if the pages be announced so that the congregation can find them in the Prayer Book. Often a prayer takes on new reality when it is not only heard with the ear, but joined in vocally. Many have found this as they have used the Series II Holy Communion rite.

In my own parish church at Bishopthorpe some time back, I shared in a service in which, under the direction of the Vicar, an interesting experiment took place. It was a service in which several congregations had combined, and the Vicar had arranged that, in the period for prayer before the sermon, various members of the congregation, duly warned and helped beforehand, should rise and lead the prayers of the people. There was something extremely real about those few minutes of worship, perhaps the more so because some, if not all, of those who led the prayers had never done so before. Their offering was costly.

It is of help if members of a congregation will let

the clergy know the matters which they want them to incorporate in the intercessions – their special causes for thanksgiving, their needs and perplexities, their sick friends, and so on. Sometimes a request can be simply expressed by the member himself who will add some such suffrage as 'Lord, hear our prayer' or 'Lord, hear us', to which the congregation will make the appropriate response. This can also be done in small, informal house-groups, where people too nervous, at least at first, to utter prayer by themselves in church, find a new reality to their praying when it is done in the intimacy of a group of perhaps half a dozen friends.

What are we to say about family prayers? Are we to dismiss this as something characteristic of the life of the Victorian, or perhaps the Edwardian, era, and just as much a thing of the past? Is it to be regarded with a kind of good-humoured nostalgia, the relic of a by-gone era, when father gathered the family round him and the maids sat lined up demurely near the dining-room door? I hope we may think again before we abandon the idea entirely. I know the difficulties; they are many and considerable – the pace of modern life, the different times at which the various members of the family leave the house, the diffidence of the ordinary Englishman to 'make a parade' of his religion, and so on. I would only say this: the responsibility of the parent for the spiritual welfare of the children is one which cannot be delegated to others without very great loss. The idea of the father as the priest of the household is one of immense value. I believe it to be true that 'the family which prays together stays together', and the impression made on the young by family prayer is not readily eradicated in later life. It may or may not be possible to have such prayer every day. It will have to be simpler and shorter than that which our grandparents knew. But I plead for an increase – a big increase – in the number of homes where it is not uncommon for father and/or mother to gather the children round them and briefly, as a family, to wait on God. Further, I plead for help from the clergy for those families who would like to experiment with this very real means of grace; this might well form the theme for useful discussion, with the help of the laity, and it might also lead to the production of printed helps to this end.

When I was in South Africa last year I learned from those who had known him of the greatness of a man I had only known through reading, Geoffrey Clayton, Archbishop of South Africa from 1949 to 1957. This was a period of severe testing for the Church, when governmental pressure made loyalty to the Christian ethic and to the dictates of Christian conscience exceedingly difficult and costly. There was something rock-like in the character of the man who late in life was called to lead the Church during that decade. On my return home I bought and read a book called *Where We Stand* (O.U.P., 1960, 8s. 6d.), which is a selection of the Charges which Archbishop Clayton delivered during that period. I close with two paragraphs from a charge given to his Diocesan Synod in 1953, and with two sentences of my own by way of comment on those paragraphs. The first paragraph is addressed to the laity:

'My brethren of the laity. Yours is the harder part. We clergymen are expected to be good. Public opinion is scandalized if we aren't. But you live in the world as we don't. For you, faithfulness means being different. I thank God for your loyalty and faithfulness. You are the strength of the Church. But you must go forward or the salt will lose its savour. There are three sides of religion: the institutional – there you help us tremendously by your generosity and by your service; there is the mystical side – that means your prayers, your worship, and your communions: probably none of you is altogether satisfied with that. God forbid that you should be. And there is the intellectual side. I do suggest that there is your greatest weakness. In every parish there should be people thinking and talking together, trying to see the practical implications of their faith.'

The second paragraph is addressed to the clergy:

'My brethren of the clergy. You set out with high ideals. You have often been disappointed. The things you wanted have not happened. Well, there was no promise that they would. There are two great commandments, the love of God and the love of neighbour. Don't try to live on the love of neighbour. It is because you can't do that that you need retreats and such things. It is only the love of God that will save you from growing sour and cynical, or content with secular compensations. You can't live on the love of neighbour. You can live on the love of God.'

So much for Geoffrey Clayton. And the comment is this: 'Love of God' – yes, the Archbishop put his finger, with faultless accuracy, on what matters most. And the soil in which that love grows and flourishes is the soil of prayer.

3

REALITY IN WORSHIP

(Hebrews iv, 14–16; x, 19–25)

THERE is a striking passage in one of St. Paul's letters (1 Corinthians xiv, 24–25) in which he pictures some uninstructed or unbelieving visitor coming into the place where the Christians are gathered at worship, hearing 'something that searches his conscience and brings conviction', and so the secrets of his heart are laid bare. He falls down and worships God, crying, 'God is certainly among you.'

This, the conversion of the outsider, it may readily be admitted, is not the primary purpose of public worship. But it is a result greatly to be desired. And, I would suggest, it is one of the tests by which live worship may be assessed. It is not to be expected that the unbeliever will *understand* all that goes on in the worship of the people of God. How could he? There is a language which only those whose faces are set Zion-wards have to learn. There are family secrets, joys, and sorrows, which are only for members of the family. Let all this be granted. The point which St. Paul makes and which I believe is as relevant now as it was for Corinth in A.D. 55 is this – there should be something about Christian worship which is self-authenticating, which by its very nature and quality says even to the unbeliever: '*God is here*, in the midst of His people.'

41

In fact, the divine Presence is so manifest, so real, that it leads to man's self-abasement ('he falls down') and to his doing, perhaps for the first time in his life, what he was created for ('he worships God').

It is a highly attractive picture. I doubt whether a more important procedure for the next meeting of our parochial church council could be devised than this: the chairman would read the two verses from 1 Corinthians xiv, 24–25, to which I have referred. Silence would be kept for ten minutes while members of the parochial church council meditated on the passage. The question would then be asked: 'Is the worship of our parish church such that, if an outsider drifted in, he would be likely to be similarly moved? If not, why not? And what shall we do about it?' Any parochial church council which ventured into this arena would be likely to have some hard thinking, straight talking, and courageous acting ahead of it.

The thing that 'got' this man, this unbeliever, was the sense of *God in the midst* – the theologians would call it the sense of the numinous. How define the indefinable? Some of the things most impossible of definition are in fact the most real. So was this. Was it a sense of joy on the part of the worshippers that they were allowed to be in the presence of God –

> *redeemed, restored, forgiven,*
> *through Jesus' precious blood?*

Was it a sense of awe which could only find expression in silence? Was it the sheer delight of finding new truth dawning on them through the exposition of the Gospel? Was it their sense of acceptance by God and by one another, sacramentally expressed in the Eucharist? Was it something of *all* these, fused together? We cannot tell. God was in the midst. That was enough. This man fell down. He worshipped.

This sense of the numinous, of the presence of God, cannot be artificially induced. But it can easily be blocked. If, for example, the service sounds like one long dirge, the hymns dragged, the Psalms murdered because the congregation (? and choir) does not know how to point them, the parson's voice somewhat minor in key, how shall this service speak of the One whose main cry on earth seems to have been 'Be of good cheer', and whose parting gift to His disciples was a joy the like of which the world had never seen? Or again, if no time be allowed for silence, if no chance be given for God to speak to us because we are engaged in a non-stop broadcast to Him, if there is no let-up from the voice of priest or Reader, is it not likely that we shall ourselves be guilty of blocking the sense of the divine presence? (I see that the anonymous, but very percipient, Editor of Crockford's Clerical Directory, 1968 edition, in commenting on the Series II Holy Communion Service, notes, rightly or wrongly, a lack of *mystery*, and pleads for a period of silence at the end of the Thanksgiving (*Preface*, p. ix). I would add a plea that during the administration of the elements, there should be absolute quiet; if there must be music, it should be so hushed as to be only just audible.)

Perhaps it was more than coincidence that, within a few days of writing this last paragraph, in the ordinary course of my diocesan work I fell into conversation with a churchwarden. He was a man of nearly seventy. I had just celebrated the Holy Communion according to the Series II rite. 'The trouble with the new services,' he said, 'is that they seem to have taken away the sense of mystery.' He then added: 'We need more silence. I suffered a great bereavement, and at that time I discovered the value of silence during worship.' I make no comment. I simply record the thoughts of a wise layman disclosed to me just at the moment when these matters of mystery and of silence were uppermost in my mind.

Rudolf Otto, in his *The Idea of the Holy*, has a significant passage on silence. He writes:

'Not even music, which else can give manifold expression to all the feelings of the mind, has any positive way to express "the holy". Even the most consummate Mass music can only give utterance to the holiest, most numinous moment in the Mass – the moment of transubstantiation – by sinking into stillness: no mere momentary pause, but an absolute cessation of sound long enough for us to "hear the silence" itself; and no devotional moment in the whole Mass approximates in impressiveness to this "keeping silence before the Lord" ' (p. 85).

There is an interesting parallel in the realm of sculpture. *An Artist and the Pope* (Peter Davies, 1969) is the story of the friendship which grew up between Pope John XXIII and Giacomo Manzù, the artist who made several busts of the Pope and eventually his death-mask. He also made the great doors for St. Peter's, Rome. I quote two sentences from the book: 'Manzù often worked harder to create the silent intervals, the voids, than he did the spaces which were to be filled with sculpture. For as in music where the weight of silence can equal that of sound, so in sculpture do empty voids balance full forms' (p. 158). Those two sentences, if pondered and acted on by those of us who are responsible for the conduct of the liturgical worship of the Church, might make all the difference between noisy formality and awe-inspiring reality.

Yes, the sense of the numinous can easily be blocked. The use of new services by itself will not induce it. It goes far deeper than that. It lies somewhere in the region of that wonder on the part of the Christian which is akin to worship and that gratitude to God for creation and redemption which seeks to make as worthy a response as is possible, with the aid of the ever-present and ever-blessed Spirit.

Perhaps part of our difficulty in worship springs not only from the fact that – to use the title of one of J. B. Phillips' books – 'our God is too small', but also from the fact that our concept of worship is too small. Naturally enough, we tend to think in terms of the little group of people who gather Sunday by Sunday in our local church, so well known to us, such a strange mixture of saints and sinners and everything in between; the not very expert organist and the man in the choir whose voice – well, the less said the better. But what in fact are we doing? Whenever we worship we join 'with angels and archangels and with all the company of heaven'. So we are not alone, nor simply in the presence of the little local group. No; we are caught up into the company of the whole Church of

God, militant and triumphant. Canon Basil Moss has put it well:

> 'I'm fed up with this ghastly picture of prayer as a private telephone line with or without a voice at the other end. It's much more like you and me playing our second fiddles in an unending heavenly orchestral symphony of praise and joy. When we pray, we take up our fiddles, and when we stop we put them down again – but the music never stops' (*Spirituality for Today*, ed. Eric James, p. 161).

This helps us to see worship in its proper context.

Much of what I have said so far amounts to a plea for reality in worship, honest-to-goodness, down-to-earth, reality which the uninstructed 'outsider' will recognise for what it is, *real* worship of *real* people at grips with a *real* God, using their wits, and using all that the devotion of saints and scholars has given them for their help.

Let me mention several parts of our worship which call for scrutiny under the searching lamp of reality.

I mention first, and very briefly, the common practice of monotoning parts of the services. Has not the time come when we should ask ourselves what is gained by *monotoning* the prayers or, for that matter, monotoning that great affirmation of our faith, the Creed? Yes, of course, that was right in a vast building before there were any amplifying aids. But why in an ordinary parish church to-day? Does it make for reality? Does God prefer it that way? I doubt it. I hope I shall not be accused of irreverence if I add I am quite sure

He does not when the man doing it cannot keep a note, and I doubt it even when he can. Does monotoning help the people to 'draw near', as the New Testament puts it, 'in full assurance of faith', or does it, rather, encourage wandering thoughts and – boredom?

I pass on to the matter of singing the Psalms. 'Oh, don't say the Archbishop is going to rob us of this,' I hear someone say. And I reply: 'I am only asking you to scrutinise this not inconsiderable part of Anglican worship in the light of *reality in worship*.' Let us face it – this is for the ordinary choir a very difficult operation; and if this is so for the choir, how much more for the ordinary member of the congregation. I speak as one who loves to hear the Psalms well sung and who has often accompanied them on organ and piano. I speak as one who is an enthusiast for the kind of speech-rhythm approach with which the Royal School of Church Music has made us familiar and which has done so much to enliven and beautify the worship of our churches. I speak as one who derives immense pleasure – and I hope profit – from listening to the choir of York Minster or of a good parish church singing the Psalms really well and with an ease born of long practice. But I also speak as a diocesan bishop who travels constantly up and down his diocese to churches of all kinds where, for all the gallant attempts of organist and choir-master (and, often, of Vicar), the effort is, frankly, too much for them; and as for the congregation, they are either left out almost completely or are reduced to a timid murmur – they do not know how to do it, and they are not going to make public fools of themselves (and who is to blame them?). So they resign themselves to silence or near-silence, and to the hope that it will soon be over.

By way of contrast, let me tell you a story. Some years ago, when Coventry Cathedral was still in process of building, I dropped in one Sunday morning on a journey from South to North. Services were being held in a hall in what is now the basement of the Cathedral – I believe that part of the building is now used for stores. There was no beauty that we should desire it. The shape of the building was wrong – all the 'aesthetics' were wrong. There was no organ – only a piano. But a wise man was in charge of the worship – Joseph Poole who, before he went to Coventry, had done so much to make the worship of Canterbury Cathedral the thing of beauty that it was, and is. The service was Mattins. When it came to the Psalms, this is what he did. He asked us all to sit. He gave us time to settle down. He announced the Psalm, and gave us ample time to find the place. Then, slowly, clearly, meaningfully, he read one verse and we, leisurely and in full throat, read the next. So it went on until, at the end, we stood for the *Gloria*. It was a fine piece of intelligent congregational worship, far, far more effective than the pathetic attempt to sing, often to a tune above the reach of our straining vocal chords, words which we have no idea how to fit into the appointed chant.

I touch now, very briefly, on other points which make for reality in public worship. *Timing* is very important. I take it for granted that none of us will be guilty of the near-blasphemy of a hurried, gabbled, or inaudible service. This causes grave offence to the laity. It is not an easy art to get our timing right – to keep a service moving, never to let it drag, but to allow ample time for people to rise, sit, kneel, find their places, before the next item in the act of worship begins. For example, are we all guiltless of beginning the *Gloria* after the opening versicles and responses of Mattins or Evensong before the people have risen from their knees and are ready for it?

Again, the Lord's Prayer used more than once in a service does not make for reality but for vain repetition (Series II Holy Communion, Mattins and Evensong avoid this pitfall). The oft-repeated 'The Lord be with you' edifies no one. (Even Series II Holy Communion is guilty of having it three times in addition to 'The peace of the Lord be always with you'.) The fussy announcing of Psalms is wearisome. Thus: is it necessary to say, Psalm 23, which is the second Psalm appointed for the 4th evening of the month, Psalm 23? If our people can find the Psalms in the Prayer Book at all, surely they can find the 23rd. It is, therefore, only necessary to announce once, clearly, 'Psalm 23', – and we may and should leave it at that.

Amens sung after prayers *said* are, of course, a liturgical abomination. And why should we have *Amens* at all at the end of hymns? They achieve little if anything, and generally are dragged. They do not make for reality. Nor do hymns and chants pitched too high. Your organist need not be able to transpose; you have only to provide him with a hymn book or chant book in which the tunes and chants are lowered for him to make congregational participation and enjoyment possible.* And getting off to a good start is vital. If the priest or Reader says: 'Let the congregation stand,' and only when they have done so, announces the hymn, the chances are that the congregation will be able to begin on line one, word one, rather than come in about line three!

As we vigilantly keep guard over our conduct of worship, so we need to help our people in this great and demanding task. We must steadily teach them that it is no mark of reverence to mutter or murmur – awe in the presence of God does not demand an unnatural approach to our heavenly Father. Congregational worship (*common* prayer) should be seen and heard for what it is – the whole family joining in with heart and mind and *voice*. The cleansed leper '*with a loud voice* glorified God' – good man! A congregation can kindle the flame of worship – or quench it!

Again, turn the searchlight of reality in worship on to the subject of the *reading of the Lessons*, whether at Mattins, Evensong, or Holy Communion. This is surely one of the most important parts of divine worship. May I be forgiven if I make the point that not one of us knows his Bible so well that he does not need to prepare the Lessons afresh *every time* he has the immense privilege of reading them? And should I be wrong if I made the point that generally they are read much too fast? The truths in them are meant to *register*, and registering takes time in our slow minds.

*The *Ancient and Modern Revised* has lower hymn settings (William Clowes & Sons, Ltd., 14 Lower Regent Street, S.W.1., 25s). The *Oxford Chant Book No. 1* (for Sundays) has few high-reciting notes (Oxford University Press, Ely House, 37 Dover Street, W.1., 15s).

Dear reader, wait a brief moment till the point sinks in, give the seed a chance to settle into the earth, before you speed on! Pauses are powerful.

The method of announcement of the Lessons is not too trivial to call for mention. It is to be hoped that we encourage our people, if so they will, to follow the Lessons in the Bibles which they bring or we provide. This is a habit much to be desired, for thus use is made of both eye-gate and ear-gate for the entrance of truth. We should, then, announce the Lesson thus: 'The book of the prophet Isaiah, chapter 40, (beginning at) verse 12' – first the book, then the chapter, then the verse (if it be other than the first verse).

And I believe that, unless the passage read is such as conveys its message easily to a non-Biblically-minded generation, the Lesson should be prefaced by two or three very carefully prepared sentences of introduction. If the Lesson plunges into the middle of an historical passage or a prophetic chapter the understanding of which depends on some knowledge of the context, then it is up to the reader to provide that context. What is the use of reading some abstruse passage from the prophets unless the reader help the listener to understand what it is all about? I am not asking for a sermonette. The reader must exercise stern discipline in keeping his comment crisp. He is the best man to provide that comment, for he knows his people and can judge what sort of comment will help them most. But if he thinks himself unable to produce such comments, then there are books which will do the work for him. I think, for example, of *Headings for the Lessons*, by Bishop H. de Candole (Mowbrays, 10*s*. 6*d*.) and *Here Beginneth*

(Pergamon Press (R.E.P.), 10*s*. 6*d*.).

From what version(s) should he read? The legal position is made clear in the *Prayer Book* (*Versions of the Bible*) *Measure 1965*. There is perfect freedom to read those lections which are not printed in the services in the Book of Common Prayer in any version we choose. This applies, for example, to Mattins and Evensong. But in such services as Holy Communion, where the Gospels and Epistles are printed, or in the Baptism Service where the Gospel is, the Church of England has decided through its Convocations that any of the following may be used (providing the parochial church council agrees) – the Authorised Version, the Revised Version, the Revised Standard Version, the New English Bible New Testament. The New English Bible Old Testament is due out early in 1970, and it is to be expected that the Convocations will be asked to authorise the Old Testament as they have done the New. So much for the legal position. But what in fact should the parish priest do with this considerable liberty which is now his? Should he use it, accustoming his people to hearing the ancient Scriptures in a modern version? Or should he retain the old rhythms and cadences of the 1611 Version? The answer to that question will depend on what you think the reading of the Lessons is for – on what reaction you hope for as a result of the reading. If you want the people to say: 'Wasn't that beautiful – what matchless language those Elizabethans wrote!', then there is but one version for you to use; the (so-called) Authorised Version has lain on the lectern for centuries; it must lie there still. And you may reassure yourself by asserting – what I believe is undeniably true – that no generation since that of 1611 has been able to produce a version as lovely to the ear as this. But if, on the other hand, you seek for a different reaction from your people; if you hope and pray that the reading of the Scriptures will be a door through which a word from the living God will come to them; if you seek for them, as for yourself, a blow at the heart and a blush on the cheek as a result of God's sword-thrust through His word, then I have little doubt what your action should be. You should seek the goodwill of your parochial church council to read to your people from a modern version, not so lovely as the old (let that be granted) but, by the very modernity of its language and by its use of innumerable finds of Biblical scholarship, conveying, as no ancient translation can, the message of the Bible to a modern of the late twentieth century.

I have little doubt as to which is the right course of action. The prophet Ezekiel once complained that, to the people who thronged to hear him, he was 'like a love-song beautifully sung to music. They listen to your words, but no one puts them into practice' (Ezekiel xxxiii, 32). The effect of the reading of Scripture is not to be compared to the effect of a love-song beautifully sung to music. No. It is to provide a means by which the living word of the living God confronts and challenges His people. Let it loose, I say, unfettered by the shackles which the passing of the centuries is bound to have put upon it.

The present generation of churchmen is extraordinarily fortunate in the wealth of material available to help it in reality of worship. Not only have we these modern versions of the Bible which enshrine the best of world scholarship of recent decades. We have also the Revised Psalter which, while retaining the cadences of Coverdale (T. S. Eliot and C. S. Lewis saw to that) does away with his ignorances and occasional absurdities.* We have a Revised Catechism which brings up to date the Catechism of the Prayer Book and fills in many of its lacunae. We have new services which it is up to us to try out patiently and with open minds, alert to what is good in the efforts of the liturgiologists, aware of the fact that new shoes sometimes pinch and only become comfortable when we have worn them for quite a while!

'Reality in worship' – that has been my theme. I can imagine that some may criticise what I have said as being, in part at least, trivial – 'fancy trying to teach us how to announce the Lessons!' But it is in the little things that we so often fall down. And God, it would seem, was interested not only in making the galaxies of the heavens but also in fashioning the patterns of the snow-flakes. It is time for a review of the conduct of our public worship. Worship, like theology, is *semper reformanda*.

* *The Revised Parish Psalter* (with chants) (Faith Press, 7 Tufton Street, S.W.1, 21s.). Also pew edition (printed) 8s. 6d. Also bound up with the Book of Common Prayer, 10s. 6d.

4

PROCLAIMING THE FAITH

(1 Corinthians i, 25–ii, 5)

THERE are many ways of proclaiming the Faith of
Jesus Christ. The most mighty proclamation is the
wordless witness of a consistently holy life. St. Peter
refers to this when he writes to Christian women who
have unbelieving husbands. He envisages their being
'won over, without a word being said, by observing the
chaste and reverent behaviour of their wives' (1 Peter iii,
1). 'What you are speaks so loud that I cannot hear
what you say' – that is terrifyingly true.

There is the proclamation of Christian compassion
which drives men and women to forsake ease and for
Christ's sake to minister to His brethren in need. It
may be Father Damien, binding up the rotting limbs
of the lepers until one day, after Mass, he turned to
them and addressed them no longer as 'my brethren',
but included himself with them in the telling phrase 'we
lepers'. It may be Schweitzer, doctor of philosophy, of
divinity, of music, and of medicine, leaving all the
prizes of Europe for Lambarene. It may be a person
refusing a pleasant job because he cannot bring himself to leave Christ's underprivileged in Hull or
Middlesbrough – we have got such men in this diocese.
It may be a nurse giving her skill in Vietnam or

Biafra because the love of Christ constrains her. This is Christian proclamation.

There is the proclamation made possible by the meeting together of kindred minds and hearts in study and prayer. I have noticed a growing desire for this in this diocese in recent months. There is, of course, nothing new in this. It is as old as Christianity itself. St. Luke tells of one such group. The leader of the group was Jesus Himself. The subject of study was what we call the Old Testament (St. Luke xxiv, 27). The result of the study was opened eyes and burning hearts (v. 32) and a verbal proclamation of the resurrection of Jesus (vv. 33–35). Groups like this are springing up in many places, not by any means always led by the clergy. (Do we clergy sometimes tend to monopolise the conversation, and should we more often leave the laity to get on with it, only coming in when we are needed and called for?) Out of such groups of mentally alert men and women, searching for truth and further light, is often born the desire to pass on what is discovered or, rather, to make known Him who reveals Himself in the group – and that is Christian proclamation.

There is a different kind of group out of which may come Christian proclamation. I am thinking of a mixed group of committed Christians and of others who are enquiring as to the truth of Christianity or who are even actively opposed to it. Here are men and women engaged in serious dialogue. The demands made on the Christian members of the group are very considerable. They must be humble enough really to *listen* to what the non-Christian members of the group have to say, and to *learn* from them. If all your life you have assumed the truth of Christianity and have sought to regulate your conduct by it, it is not easy to get alongside, to enter into the thought-forms of the man who has never believed it or who, having once held it, has thrown it over. The ability never (repeat never) to be shocked but eagerly to understand the approach of the enquirer or of the antagonist is a gift much to be desired. Such an enquirer or antagonist is likely to listen to us only when he sees that his Christian opposite number is a humble learner. Only then can anything like proclamation begin.

I have touched on various forms of proclamation. Now I come to the proclamation made through preaching, and to it I devote the major part of this address. I do so only after considerable hesitation, for I have written and spoken a good deal on this subject, as many of you know. But I revert to the theme here because 'I can no other'; the subject is hot within me – and will out!

I have noticed – and you, no doubt have, too – in recent years a very marked loss of nerve on the part of clergy, deaconesses, Readers, and others who are entrusted with the ministry of the word. It would be easy to diagnose the causes of this loss of nerve. I shall touch on only a few of them here – and that briefly.

It is often said that the general atmosphere of the late twentieth century is inimical to the ministry of preaching, and there is much truth in this. The neat and tidy little world of the Victorian era, with its hopeful vision of human progress and of Utopia round the corner, has been split wide open. Not only have two world wars shaken our complacency, but the very toughness of the ills which assault us presents us with the gravest possible moral problems. Why is it, for example, that in an age of immense scientific advance the problems of war and famine and disease prove so intractable? Further, our horizons are stretched almost beyond human endurance by scientific discoveries and by technological achievements. How comfortable, we think, it must have been in the days before Galileo to think of the world as the centre of everything, or, with Archbishop Ussher, to be able to fix a date for the creation! But all this is long gone, and we must think in terms of millions of light years and of our advance to the moon as but the first timid step of a child-race learning to come to terms with the planets. Where does the God of the Victorians – or of the Bible – come into this? Should we abandon the God we thought we once knew and, bowing before the techno-crats, cry 'These be thy gods, O moderns'?

Nor has much recent theology made the preacher's task more easy. If Karl Barth, with his tremendous affirmation of the transcendence of God and of His revelation of Himself in Jesus Christ and the Word of God, sounded a trumpet which preachers might in their turn take up, he was followed by others whose emphasis on demythologisation raised many questions for the preacher. Is it possible to preach with conviction and power Christ crucified and risen if in fact He never rose?* And so on. The questions with which the theologians were wrestling were popularised in

* On this see Bishop Stephen Neill, *The Interpretation of the New Testament 1861–1961*, chapter 6, especially pp. 222–235.

paperbacks (the sale of Bishop John A. T. Robinson's *Honest to God* has run into over a million copies) and were brought into our homes by discussion (often very confused and badly presented) on radio and television. The man in the street became familiar with catch phrases like 'man come of age', 'the man for others', 'religionless Christianity', very often without understanding the origin of those phrases and without more than an inkling of the kind of life lived, for example, by Dietrich Bonhoeffer with whom some of the phrases originated or by whom they were made popular (see further, p. 31 ff.). Equipped often with little more than a smattering of the topical phrases, the man in the street has felt uneasy and wondered whether, after all, the kind of Christianity which the Church presents (or which he thinks the Church presents) is not hopelessly outmoded and is best discarded as belonging to the infant stage of our development.

The position is made the more difficult in that ours is a *headline* age. We skip lightly through our newspapers. We glance at the pictures which flash on our television screen. We are like bees, extracting a little here and a little there, but never staying in one place for long. We are not good at concentration, at following a line of thought through. We ask how on earth our grandfathers could stomach Liddon or Spurgeon.

These and a dozen other causes within and without the Church make the preacher's task difficult. One needs a very firm conviction of the truth of one's message and of man's desperate need for it if these difficulties are to be seen for what in fact they are – challenges to be met, to be faced, to be answered. It is very easy to heed the parrot cry, shallow and superficial though I believe it to be, which says 'The day of preaching is over.' Let this be repeated often enough – and the prophets of woe seem to take an almost sadistic delight in repeating it – and, like a germ, it will enter our system and devitalise us. And then our Father Below, as C. S. Lewis used to call the Devil, chalks up another success and laughs up his ample sleeve.

Then there are those who speak of 'Christian presence' in the world – the phrase recurs very frequently in recent writing – as being almost the only form of witness to Jesus Christ which is allowable in modern society. The word 'God' or the name of Jesus Christ must be used with the utmost caution – better not to use it at all than to incur the risk of misunderstanding from a generation which finds it very hard to give any kind of valid content to such an idea. So it is said. But is this true? Can this not all too easily produce the situation described by a twenty-year-old college girl who for several weeks visited a number of churches and then reported to her mother : 'I heard about everything from abortion to the war in Vietnam. I had hoped to hear something about God'?

Some time back a conference was held in Oxford and preaching was being discussed. The point was made that the day of authoritarian sermons was passed; we must present the Gospel in terms acceptable to the questioning temper of our age and not simply throw texts or dogmas at people as if they were above debate. An Oxford philosopher demurred. Of course he did not want texts thrown at him. But he wanted to hear a word of real authority, not just qualified propositions, from the preacher. The word of the Lord is a word from God and a word about God – the preacher is failing in his duty if he does not present to his people the great affirmations of the Gospel. It may be that to many modern ears the words of Malachi sound too authoritarian a note, but nonetheless they deserve the most serious pondering: 'A priest's lips should transmit knowledge, so that men may seek rulings from him, because he is the messenger of the Lord of Hosts,' (Malachi ii, 7).

The Reverend Colin Hickling makes the point with sensitiveness in an essay contributed to a recent book *Church without Walls*:

'Theology is what we stand for. For theology interprets Christ. We aspire, naturally, to render Christ and his redemption effectively present in our society. We aspire to do so, in these days perhaps a little too self-consciously, through the contribution we may be enabled to make at many practical points to the well-being of the world. With all this we are very familiar. But this redeeming activity of God in us needs interpreting. There is a place for proclamation, even though it may be made in a quieter tone of voice than that word indicates. And the quieter, the more reasoned and personal, the tone of communication, the more essentially it must become one of theology. How rightly the Lutherans refer to their pastors and ministerial candidates as "theologians" ' (pp. 109–110).

More serious, I think, than the cry 'the day of preaching is over' or the appeal to 'the Christian presence'

61

as the only valid form of proclamation, is the cry, sometimes easily uttered, sometimes wrung from the preacher in an agony of soul, 'I haven't got the gift. Other gifts I may have, but not the gift of preaching. That has been denied me. And yet, I am expected to get up week in, week out and address my congregation.' With the man who utters that cry in real distress I have the deepest sympathy. God in His wisdom has dispersed His gifts with lavish hand, but He has dispersed them widely – 'there are diversities of gifts'; that is good New Testament doctrine (see, e.g. Romans xii; 1 Corinthians xii, and Ephesians iv). There is no doubt that to some He has given the gift of preaching in a special way. It is not necessarily true that to such a man preaching comes easily; it may *seem* to do so, but *ars est celare artem* and the smoothest-flowing and most powerful preaching is often the result of long hours of toil and study and prayer. But there *are* men who are gifted above others with the ability to expound, to apply, to interest in a way denied to others. Let that be granted. But if I am clearly not one of this class, what then? Consider what preaching is. When I taught in a theological college, I used to set the students a question: 'What is preaching?' Great was the variety of answers which I received. And small wonder, for the question is not patient of an easy and pat answer. (Phillips Brooks' definition of preaching as 'the communication of truth by man to men', always seems to me to be woefully inadequate.) But one answer is this: 'Preaching is the overflow of a man's religion.' I take that answer to mean this: if a man's heart is full of the love of God, if his mind has been full of the things of God during the week, if he has been feeding on the message of God, if he has been in touch with the needs of his people, then, provided he is prepared to work hard, he should not find it too difficult week by week to speak to his congregation of the things of God. Rather, he should look forward to his entry into the pulpit each Sunday as an opportunity to show his people some further facet of the many-splendoured grace of God. He will, of course, need help, over and above that of his reading. He would do well to seek a place on one of the courses provided by the College of Preachers (All Saints' Hall, Ennismore Gardens, London, S.W.7.) which exist for the one purpose of bringing aid to men who take their preaching work seriously. He should from time to time read other men's sermons to see how they approach their task. He should join with some of his clerical neighbours in joint preparation, so that mind may sharpen mind and mutual enrichment ensue. He is not meant, within the fellowship of Christ's Church, to labour on entirely alone and unaided. But, given this aid and given the willingness to be aided, preaching can be, indeed should be, a joy rather than a subject of dread.

I turn now to a matter which has for long been troubling me a good deal and I am anxious not to be misunderstood. The old pattern of Sunday worship – 8.00 a.m. Holy Communion, 11.00 a.m. Mattins, 6.30 p.m. Evensong – was good for the middle and upper classes of Victorian and Edwardian days and even for the days of George V. But that pattern has gone for ever in Britain. Gone also – except for a minority – is the habit of going to Church more than once a Sunday

– more's the pity, but it is a fact. Mattins and Evensong persist in many churches as the main services of the day; but I think it would be true to say that in the great majority the main service of the day is the Family Eucharist, generally held at, say, 9.30 or 10.00 a.m. Evensong has not been abandoned, as it has on the other side of the Atlantic. Sometimes it is well attended, sometimes badly. In the restoration of the Eucharist to its proper place in the worship of the Church we can unfeignedly rejoice – we seem to be recovering the New Testament pattern whereby the Lord's people met on the Lord's day around the Lord's Table. Thank God for that. But before we sit back at ease in Sion, satisfied with this liturgical achievement, let us ask one or two questions. Exactly how many minutes at each Eucharist are devoted to the preaching of the Word? The truthful answer to that will generally be 'seven to ten minutes'. Sometimes it is five. Sometimes (not often?) fifteen. Next question: What is the theme of the weekly preaching? The answer is generally: the Gospel of the day. But what of the Epistles? Or, if the answer be, sometimes the Gospel, sometimes the Epistle, I ask: What continuity of teaching is there? Next question: How often do you expound the Old Testament to your people? I know – and I rejoice in the fact – that provision is made in the Series II Holy Communion Service for an Old Testament lection. But in what proportion of our churches is advantage taken of this provision, and *even in them,* how often is this the basis of the sermon? I am glad to note that, in *The Calendar and Lessons for the Church's Year* (A Report submitted by the Church of England

Liturgical Commission to the Archbishops of Canterbury and York, S.P.C.K., 1969, 10s. 6d.), the proposed Eucharistic Lectionary 'implies that, if only two lessons are desired, the Old Testament shall have preference over the Epistle in the pre-Christmas period . . .' (p. 7). Very wisely, the Commission notes:

'The desirability of a fuller acquaintance with the Old Testament is widely recognised – especially for congregations hearing only New Testament Epistles and Gospels at Holy Communion – as a proper and necessary background to a full understanding of Christ and the Gospel. The Old Testament lessons are designed to give depth to the New Testament readings, and it is greatly to be hoped that experiment will be made in using them' (p. 8).

Now I believe that these questions are of fundamental importance. Let us take a typical instance of the kind of person I have in mind. Here is a young banker (farmer, housewife, I.C.I. worker). He is fairly regular at church, attending only once a week and that at the Family Eucharist. He learnt very little at school about the Christian Faith, a bit more at Confirmation classes (though that is pretty dim now in his memory). At his work he is in an atmosphere hostile to Christianity. He feels the need of being equipped for what is very really a battle – moral and intellectual. Sunday by Sunday he receives sacramental grace. But he needs also to be *taught* – and he wants to be taught – how else can he meet the questions and the taunts of his colleagues? A few thoughts on the Gospel of the day just will not do. Slowly, steadily, systematically, intelligently, he must be taught the Faith – Gospels, Epistles, Old Testament, the relevance of their central doctrines to life, until, over the years, something of the 'wholeness' of Christianity begins to dawn on him. If he does not get this on Sunday morning at nine-thirty, he will not get it anywhere else. The truth is as stark as that! *Is he getting it?*

These questions have been raised from time to time in various quarters, but have they been seriously faced and adequately answered? I doubt it. If we continue to bypass them, let us at least do so with our eyes open to the results which assuredly will follow. We shall be responsible for a generation of Christians, untaught, uninstructed, ill-equipped to meet the questions which are being asked about Christianity, silent because they know they will be worsted in argument when they should be armed to do battle for the Faith. And this at a time when, the number of committed Christians being small in relation to the population, it is all the more vital that that minority should be trained, alert, and ready for action.

I sound this warning note, and suggest that there are few tasks of greater importance for the leaders of our parochial worship than to get together in local groups and – not discuss the problem and its undoubted difficulties but – make definite plans for resolving it in the remaining months of 1969 and in the years ahead.

All of which leads us back to the question on which we touched: what is preaching? And on to the question: what is preaching for? Perhaps the two questions can best be approached (not answered, for they are far too big) together.

I have already criticised Phillips Brooks' definition of preaching as 'the communication of truth by man to men' (*Lectures on Preaching*, p. 5). What sort of truth? And what sort of man communicates it? – can *any* man preach? Surely not! This is a valuable definition, in so far as it emphasises two essential elements in preaching, viz. truth and personality. But it does not get us far enough.

Would this be better as a definition: 'A man of God, face to face with men and women in need, grappling with a word from God'? Or this, from Bernard Lord Manning: 'A manifestation of the Incarnate Word, from the written word, by the spoken word.' At least this definition serves to keep the emphasis in the right place. It reminds us of the entry of John Wesley in his *Journal* for July 17th, 1739: 'I rode to Bradford five miles from Bath. Some persons had pitched on a convenient place, on the top of the hill under which the town lies; there I offered Christ to about 1,000 people, for wisdom, righteousness, sanctification and redemption.' The pregnant phrase 'I offered Christ' recalls Wesley's definition of his function as being that of 'a man sent from God to persuade men to put Jesus Christ at the centre of their relationships'.

But there is another factor which must be borne in mind when we are seeking to define preaching. It is this. Preaching is more than a human activity. It is a divine activity. It is God at work through dedicated human agency – probing, challenging mind and will, offering His succour, proffering His grace.

St. Augustine once defined the task of the speaker thus: '*Ita dicere debere eloquentem, ut doceat, ut delectat, ut flectat*' – to teach, to move, to turn. There he touched on the three parts of a man's personality which preaching should reach – his mind (*teach*), his emotions (*move*), his will (*turn*). Should there not be an element of all these three at least in most of the sermons we preach?

5

CHANGING THE POINTS – A CALL TO THE CHURCH

(St. John i, 1–5; Hebrews i, 1–3)

IT was in May 1947 that the then Archbishop of Canterbury, Dr. Geoffrey Fisher, in a speech to the Convocation of Canterbury, set in motion the revision of the Canons of 1603. They had served for more than three and a half centuries, but many were outdated and the need for revision was obvious. For over twenty years the Convocations – and for a shorter time the House of Laity – have been at work on the Canons. The task is now virtually complete, and the promulging of the new Canons is expected very shortly. Every parish will receive a copy. The book should be studied especially by clergy and churchwardens, and kept for reference in the vestry. Sometimes over the years, the debates on Canon Law have been arid and one has been tempted to ask whether all this expenditure of time, energy, and money was justified. But it can rightly be replied that no great body ought to be governed by antiquated rules. We were right to revise them, and to appoint, as we have done, a committee to ensure that they are kept in good repair (The Church Assembly Canon Law Standing Commission).

It was in 1958 that the Church Assembly 'asked for

the opinion of the Convocations on various proposed ways by which the laity might be more closely associated with the clergy in the Synodical Government of the Church'. It was high time that the Church looked at its processes of government. The machinery of former years has been cumbrous enough, in all conscience. There have been the two Convocations of Canterbury and York, themselves more ancient than our secular parliamentary system, each of them with an Upper and a Lower House. Then there has been the Church Assembly, brought into being in 1919 by the Enabling Act 'to deliberate on all matters concerning the Church of England and to make provision in respect thereof'. This Assembly consists of the House of Bishops, the House of Clergy (consisting of the two Lower Houses of the Convocations) and the House of Laity. It meets three times a year. It is time-consuming and its wheels necessarily grind slowly. The amount of good work which it does is often not fully recognised, especially by those who take a short-term view of its activities and who become annoyed at some sessions the connection of whose business with the advancement of the Kingdom of God is a little hard to find! In recent years, the laity have by courtesy been given a share in the discussion of doctrinal matters such as liturgical revision, but now it is felt – and surely rightly – that this share is theirs *by right*, and Church government must be so fashioned as to give expression to this.

All this has given rise to more than a decade of debate on the central government of the Church and on its diocesan and local government too. (See especially *Government by Synod*, being the Report of the Commission appointed by the Archbishops of Canterbury and York – Church Information Office, 1966, 7s. 6d.) The fruition of this debate will shortly be seen, when, in the autumn of 1970, the first General Synod is held. The dioceses are already at work planning for the implementation locally of government by synod.

For a long time dissatisfaction has been felt and consciences have been strained by the necessity of declaring assent to the Thirty-Nine Articles. Many feel that, valuable as the Articles are as an historical document reflecting the theology and thought-forms of a particular period of Anglican history, it should not be made incumbent on clergy (and on some laity) to assent to them in the way now customary in the Church of England. The subject was raised at the 1968 Lambeth Conference, and dealt with very unsatisfactorily because of lack of time. The Bishop of Durham brought the matter before Church Assembly in February 1969, and it was referred to the Convocations. It is much to be hoped that the Convocations may see their way to move that the recommendation of the Bishop of Durham's Commission, which seemed to meet with a good deal of approval by members of the Church Assembly, be adopted. The matter is of considerable importance, and it is right that attention be given to it. (*See Subscription and Assent to the Thirty-Nine Articles*, S.P.C.K., 1968, 9s. 6d.)

All these matters may be called the *machinery* of Church government, and the word should not be used derogatorily. Machinery matters. It does no credit to the Church, nor does it bring honour to the Church's Lord, if its machinery is so antiquated or cumbersome that it creaks or breaks down. The world is rightly critical if it sees the Church run badly. We should be grateful for the lively thinking which the Church has manifested in such matters as Canon Law revision, government by synod, attention to the Declaration of Assent, and a dozen other matters.

But there is no *life* in machinery as such. Nor should machinery be the main concern of the Church. Codes of canons, and systems of government are means to an end – that is all. Even debates on Anglican–Methodist union are only means to an end – and we do well to remind ourselves that it was as long ago as 1946 that Archbishop Fisher preached his famous Cambridge sermon. Even revision of the Liturgy and experimentation with new forms of services – all of which are consuming immense stores of energy and time – are only means to an end. Perhaps the greatest danger facing the Church of England to-day is to get confused at this point, to think that these are the primary things; to get our priorities wrong.

I believe that now the time has come for us to stand back and think again. A critical moment is upon us. Our Canons are revised. Synodical government is round the corner. The irritant of a particular form of Assent may soon be removed. A decision – one way or the other – about Anglican –Methodist union is about to be reached. Liturgical revision is well under way. And so on. What are the main matters on which the Church should concentrate its thinking, its debates, its action in the decade 1970–1980?) I quote a sentence written to me in January by a Church leader: 'We have been going round and round long enough on one particular circuit and at some stage or other we need to change the points.' I believe that we have reached that stage. The Church needs to be jerked on to a different line – reorientated, to use two more of my correspondent's metaphors.

What is the line on to which we should be jerked? What ought to be the direction of our reorientation? I have little doubt in my own mind. I believe we have been concerned long enough with our own problems. The Church has been considering its own navel long enough, if the phrase be allowed. *Let it lift up its eyes and look on the fields.*

It need not look beyond the borders of these islands to see how grievous is the moral and spiritual state of the people to whom it is sent by its Master. Nor need I waste your time and mine now in elaborating the seriousness of the situation which faces us – the gap which yawns between the number of those baptised (not to say confirmed) in our Church and those who become regular worshippers in it; the small percentage of those who make any open allegiance to Christ and His claims; the rate of marriage breakdown; the increase in crime; the triviality of thinking and living of vast numbers in spite of the spread of education. One could easily, though not very profitably, go on listing signs of spiritual sickness, but they are clear for all Christian thinking men and women to see. In spite of the benefits of a Welfare State, in spite of the advantages which technology offers on all hands to the members of our society, the words of Isaiah describe our situation: 'The whole head is sick, and the whole heart faint' (i, 5).

I have no doubt that more careful diagnosis of the ills which beset us is called for, more sociological surveys, more penetrating analyses. Historians, sociologists, theologians must combine to examine the situation here in England. Much work remains to be done. But there comes a time, in the medical treatment of a patient, when diagnosis and analysis, if they are not actually stopped, must be relegated to an inferior place, and must give priority to action, a blood-transfusion or a dose of drugs or an operation. If such drastic action does not take place, the patient will die. Such a position has been reached, I believe, in the spiritual state of our nation. The time has come for evangelistic action at all levels, in all sections, even if in the doing of our evangelistic task mistakes are made. Better that than no action at all. Better that than endless consultation on the part of the doctors – while the patient breathes his last!

'But,' I shall be told, 'our people are not ready for it. First our Church people must be revived, taught, inspired. Then we may venture out to the fringers or to the completely untouched.' I have no illusions about the need of our own people for revival of spiritual life, for teaching in matters of faith and doctrine, for inspiration. The evidence of this need is all around us. But we have been told this for decades. We shall never be fully ready. Just as truth is found 'on the road' ('he who is willing to *do* God's will shall *know* of the doctrine . . .'); just as unity is found 'on the road' as we collaborate in joint activity (as well as discuss) with members of other churches; so revival of spiritual life is found 'on the road'. The best cordial for drooping spirits is to get busy on some piece of evangelistic outreach. Revival of spiritual life in the churches is more likely to come when we lift up our eyes and look on the fields of need and opportunity, and when we go into the fields to do some sweaty work there, than when we remain within the safety of our own buildings, lamenting our own spiritual state or analysing the ills of a world which has largely thrown over, if it has ever considered, the claims of Jesus Christ.

But what do we mean by the word *evangelism*? The word has been on the tongues of most churchmen, especially since 1945, when the Report *Towards the Conversion of England* came out. It is a word mistrusted by some and misunderstood by many. There can be no doubt that it was evangelism which provided the thrust to the early ecumenical movement. The leaders of the early days were inspired by the motto, 'the evangelisation of the world in this generation'. We may smile at their optimistic enthusiasm, and brand it as being naïve. We may say that the ecumenical fathers were infected by the utopianism which pervaded the thinking of the men of pre-World War I days. But when all that is said – and it is very easy to offer these criticisms – the 'first fine careless rapture' of the early years of the ecumenical movement was due to the clarity of vision of the leaders which enabled them to see that ecumenism minus evangelism was just not worth the effort – it would be dead from the start. I ask: Is the evangelisation of the world still the great passion behind the ecumenical movement, the motive force of its thinking and acting? I ask again: Is the evangelisation of our England that which provides the thrust and gives the passion to the central councils of the Church? I ask yet again: What place does the evangelisation of your parish occupy on the agenda of your parochial church council?

But to come back to the matter of definition – what do we mean by evangelism? It would be a healthy exercise for all our parochial church councils to hammer out their own definition of the word, and not to rest content until, however inadequate it was, it at least reflected some of the New Testament insights and was relevant to the local situation. It is not for me to provide a ready-made answer to the question. I simply give five phrases or sentences which are, as I think, relevant to the discussion:

(i) Canon Roger Lloyd, that percipient Church historian and shrewd observer of men, said that the task of the Church was 'to love men into taking God seriously'. That does not provide us with a definition of evangelism, but it opens up the way towards one.

(ii) 'A reconciled, forgiven Church not simply preaching but living and offering to all men the reconciliation and forgiveness of God' (J. S. Stewart: *The Wind of the Spirit*, p. 190).

(iii) 'To evangelise is so to present Jesus Christ in the power of the Holy Spirit, that men shall come to put their trust in God through Him, to accept Him as their Saviour, and serve Him as their King in the fellowship of His Church' (*Towards the Conversion of England*, p. 1).

(iv) 'Evangelism is one beggar telling another beggar

where to find bread' (or should it be 'Bread'?).

(v) 'It is the Holy Spirit who takes the Word of God and makes it a living, converting word to men. Our part in evangelism might be described as bringing about the occasions for man's response to Jesus Christ' (*The Uppsala Report 1968*; *Official Report of the Fourth Assembly of the World Council of Churches*, edited by Norman Goodall, p. 28).

These five quotations provide the Church, centrally and locally, with something of an acid test for its activities. If our debates and organisations, our planning and our discussions, are not doing something which matches, which ties in with, the above quotations, then we should question whether their demise is not to be hastened. Perhaps they have had their day, and done their work and, though good enough in themselves, should cease to engage the attention of the Church – why bother with them? A decent burial is a lovely thing.

I turn now to a matter intimately connected with the subject of evangelism. Granted that we see the need of a 'changing of the points', a radical rearrangement of our Church priorities, is it possible to be in any real sense clear as to what should be the essentials of the message we proclaim? These are days of intellectual and theological upheaval. Many theological books now appearing are much more lucid in pointing out what the Church *cannot* declare than what it *can*. A marked loss of nerve is evident when one reads or listens to the religious utterances of this decade, or views religious discussions on television. The man who ventures out with a 'thus saith the Lord' is often met with a frown or at least with a raised eyebrow. 'I venture to think that possibly . . .' is more in tune with the spirit of the age and meets with a readier response. If R. C. Moberly could speak in 1897 of a 'temper of theological hesitation and reserve' (*Ministerial Priesthood*, p. 29), how much more apposite is the phrase to-day. It is worth continuing the quotation:

> 'Under certain conditions there may be, it is true, an important place and function for the hesitating and balanced mind on questions of theology. But after all, it is not unseasonable at the present time to insist that this is only a condition of preliminary discipline. It is, after all, conviction, not balance; it is enthusiasm, not reserve; it is theological insight, not theological hesitation; it is the discernment . . . of essential principles of the theology of the Incarnation, which – all perils and pitfalls notwithstanding – is the true illumination and glory of the theologian.'

These words are as deserving of note to-day as they were at the end of last century. Perhaps they are more so.

What, then, are the sinews of the faith we proclaim in our task of evangelism? What are the essentials of our message? What can we dare to hold forth as basic certainties in an age of doubt? What, in terms of belief, do we Christians stand for?

Perhaps I shall be charged with folly in attempting even to assay an answer to these enormous questions at the end of an address. Certainly in speaking so briefly on so large a subject I lay myself open to the charge that I have left out vitally important matters

78

of belief without so much as a mention. Let me plead guilty at the start. And let me admit to the fact that what I shall now say partakes of the nature of a personal *credo*; these are the things by which I live and for which I hope – though tremblingly, for I know myself a coward – I would be prepared to die.

First, we must affirm that our God is a *God who speaks*. He has communicated and continues to communicate with His creatures. This is, perhaps, *the* essential message of the Bible, from its first page to its last, from 'Adam, where art thou?' to 'The Spirit and the Bride say "Come".' Dietrich Bonhoeffer held it to be of absolutely vital importance, that in theology man is not enquiring about God; *he is confronted by Him*. 'The serpent tempted Adam to ask a question *about* God, to treat Him as an object, something which might be handled, criticized, speculated upon. But God may only be enquired *from*. "Who are you? What are your commandments? What are you saying to us?"' (Mary Bosanquet, *The Life and Death of Dietrich Bonhoeffer*, p. 115). *God speaks.*

Secondly, we must affirm that there has been revealed a law for man, an ethic, the neglect of which will lead him to disaster. The coming of the Gospel has not meant that there is no place for the law of God. There is a grain to the universe, and we go against that grain at our peril. The Ten Commandments still hold, and it is the greatest possible pity that they are so rarely heard in our churches. The recitations of the *Kyries*, three-fold or nine-fold, does not take the place of the recitation of the law of God – *for what* are we asking the mercy of God? Obedience to the law of God is the only solid rock on which national and personal life can be built. And if, as we hear the recitation of the law, we recognise that we have sinned in the breaking of it and that we are impotent in the fulfilling of it, then the law has fulfilled its purpose, in that it has pin-pointed our weakness and put us on the road which leads to the mercy of God in Christ.

Thirdly, we must affirm that in Jesus Christ God has spoken His finally decisive word; that Jesus of Nazareth, incarnate, crucified, and risen *is* the Word of God in a unique sense – in Him the Mind and Heart and Will of God have been laid bare. In the teaching of Jesus we see the truth about God and man as no-where else. In the death and resurrection of Jesus we see the redeeming power of God at work, winning the victory over man's great enemies of sin and death. This is well summarised in the Prayer of Consecration in the Holy Communion service (Series II), where the mighty acts of God in Christ are recited – 'through Him Thou hast created all things ... through Him Thou didst redeem us ... through Him Thou hast made us a people for Thine own possession ... sending forth through Him Thy holy and life-giving Spirit'.

Fourthly, we must affirm that the Church, for all its sinfulness and its divisions, is God's chosen agent in the bringing in of His kingdom. We are conscious, as we look around us and as we read the pages of history, of the way in which the Church has failed – and still fails – her Master, and we are not oblivious of the fact that we have had our own share in that failure. But that should not lead us to a kind of morbid breast-beating which blinds us to the glory of the Church and of its achievements in the cause of Christ. A sense of proportion is called for which, if lost, is best restored by a reading of history and a liberal use of Christian biography.

So far, then, we have spoken of the voice of God, the law of God, the Word of God, and the Church as the agent of God.

Fifthly, we must affirm that the God who spake by the prophets and has worked through His Church down the centuries, still speaks and still operates by His Holy Spirit in present-day history. Nor is His activity confined to those who acknowledge the Lordship of Christ. The God who used Cyrus as His Messiah still uses those who refuse His sway. Wherever truth prevails over falsehood, and beauty over ugliness, and goodness over evil, there God is at work, and we may rejoice at the operation of His hands.

Sixthly, I have spoken elsewhere in this series of addresses of the need to affirm the social implications of the Gospel (*vide supra* p. 14 ff). A message which does not impinge – pertinently and immediately – on the problems of the day is of little use and may be roundly discounted. More than that need not be said here. That, I believe, is widely recognised but cannot be too frequently or loudly affirmed. But what I find more frequently lacking to-day is that personal allegiance and devotion to Jesus Christ which is reflected in such an old German hymn as this:

> *Thee will I love, my strength, my tower,*
> *Thee will I love, my joy, my crown,*
> *Thee will I love with all my power,*

In all my works, and Thee alone.
Thee will I love, till sacred fire
Fills my whole soul with pure desire.

Where that note is missing, our message has a hollow
sound, and our trumpet is unlikely to call many to the
battle.

PASTOR AND PEOPLE

(St. John xxi, 9–17)

THE English picture of a man of God, called, trained, set aside by ordination, spending the major part of his life in a small parish of a few hundred souls, caring for one parish church, rarely moving beyond his parish bounds – this picture smacks more of the nineteenth-century novel than of life in the last third of the twentieth century. Many things have gone to the breakdown of the traditional picture. There is the growth of the great conurbations which owe their origins to industry (in this diocese we see typical examples in Middlesbrough and Hull). There is the junction of two, three, or more parishes under the care of one Vicar – a policy undoubtedly right in itself, but which raises new problems of its own. There is the mobility of population, due to the fact that firms move their employees from place to place, with resultant problems in the education of the young and in the establishing of community relations and of religious connections and habits. Factors such as these – and there are many others – have broken up the static picture of a century or so ago. They have strained the parochial ideal almost to breaking point.

The only effective way by which that ideal can be fulfilled in a parish of 20,000 or 30,000 is by a team of workers – Vicar, woman worker(s), curate(s), social workers. Experiments in group and team ministries are much to be welcomed, for it is only by such experimentation that we shall be able to learn the lessons which we must learn if we are to penetrate the structures of city and of country life. Experiments, too, in specialist ministries are equally to be welcomed – chaplaincies for the youth, for the Universities and Colleges, for industry, for Butlin's camps, for the world of entertainment, and so on. I have no doubt that an increasing number of ordained men will find the fulfilment of their ministry in spheres which were hardly thought to be the province of the clergyman a generation or so ago.

That is all to the good. But, for all the changes, let us not lose sight of the fact that the basic work of the Church in England is still to be done by the parish priest. Not long ago, there was an article in a leading daily newspaper, entitled 'The Passing of the Parson'. I deplore the title. I do not believe for a moment that the day is past of the man whose delight it is to be in and out among his people and, as a man of God, to minister to them the things of God. To know his sheep and to be known of them, after the pattern of the great and good Shepherd, is to be entrusted with a privilege than which there is none greater.

I ask myself, then, what is required of the parish priest if he is to exercise an effective ministry. I bypass for the moment the sheer essentials of a love of God and faithfulness in private prayer and devotion (*vide supra*, chapter 2), and I mention the following:

(i) *He must be willing to stay.*

We clergy are prone to foot and mouth disease – we talk too much and we run about too much. Certainly many clergy move on too rapidly from one parish to another – they 'never continue in one stay', as the office for the Burial of the Dead so vividly puts it! The honeymoon period of the first two or three years being over, and the difficult grinding years coming on, the incumbent begins to look about him – where shall he go next? Perhaps in another parish he might find things easier and the parochial church council might be more co-operative? So it is that, just as his roots should be going down and just as he should be beginning to have the trust and love of his people, he pulls up his roots and is away. I believe that much damage can be done to the cause of the Church by clergy who are not prepared to stick it out when the going is hard, and by clergy who, having lost their spiritual and intellectual vivacity, find it necessary to move before the spiritual nakedness of their condition be seen. 'You are the men who have *stuck it through* with Me in My times of trial', Jesus is recorded as saying to His apostles (St. Luke xxii, 28). It was a high tribute. The quality of endurance occupies a surprisingly important place in the list of New Testament virtues; the subject is deserving of very careful study. The Authorised Version generally translates the Greek *hypomone* as 'patience', but the word is much more positive in meaning than that. It is the tough fibre of which the character of the saints is made. There is an impressive passage in Mary Bosanquet's *The Life and Death of Dietrich Bonhoeffer* (p. 196), in which she quotes from one of the

85

letters which the future martyr wrote to the young men in his charge at a time when their integrity was at stake and their testing under Nazi pressure was severe. The letter consisted largely of a study of the idea of patient endurance in the New Testament. 'It is noticeable how much significance the New Testament attaches to patience,' Bonhoeffer wrote. 'Only he who is patient receives the promises (Matthew 24, 13); only he who is patient truly bears fruit (Luke 8, 15). A faith which does not issue in patience is neither genuine nor effective ... Steadfastness is only proved through suffering ...' And so on. Bonhoeffer exemplified in his life and in his death the truth of which he wrote.

This willingness on the part of the parish priest to stay for a considerable period of time in a given parish should be matched on the side of the diocesan bishop and his staff by a willingness constantly to keep in mind both the need of the clergy and their families for a move and of the parishes for a change of incumbent. Any diocesan staff worth its salt is always at work on this problem, and in a happy diocese the clergy know that they can talk over their specific problems – personal, family, and parochial – with their diocesan or his advisers. Whatever our views may be of the recommendations of the authors of *Partners in Ministry,* we may be grateful for the care which the members of the Morley Commission gave to the consideration of this very important subject.

(ii) *He must be willing to visit.*

I am a great believer in visiting by teams of laymen and women, especially in our big towns and cities. In our own diocese, very worth-while experiments are going on and will, I hope, be considerably developed. Such visiting by laity in their own parishes, or by laity drafted in from one parish to another, can act as a kind of blood transfusion, and bring a real measure of new life. We have seen this in York, in Hull, and elsewhere.

But, in certain quarters, this idea of lay visiting has given rise to a heresy. It is that the clergy need not – some would say should not – visit, except in the homes of those who are members of their congregation or in cases of very special sickness or need. This heresy, like most heresies, is half truth, half lie. The half truth is that it is the duty of the laity to *be* the Church where they are, to shoulder the work of the Church, to bring the love of God in Christ to the people among whom they live. The half lie is that that exempts the clergy from visiting, exempts them, indeed, from fulfilling their ordination promise 'to *seek for* Christ's sheep which are dispersed abroad . . . that they may be saved through Christ for ever'.

I do not believe that there is anything which can take the place of a house-going parson. The old saying 'A house-going parson makes a Church-going people' may be an over-simplification in these days of complicated and sophisticated living. But there is enough truth in it still – and I believe always will be – to give us furiously to think and to provide us with guide-lines for action. This is my *credo*: I believe that nothing can compare with the pastoral and evangelistic value of a godly man, with happy face and loving heart, in and out of the homes of his people, caring for them for Christ's sake and entering into their joys and sorrows, in the places where they live and sleep. I believe that, sometimes in a muddled way and often in a way that they cannot articulate, they know – as we know – that this is one of the reasons why an ordained man is set free from office hours and from the demands made on the professional and 'working' man. When they see 'a holy man of God, passing by us continually', in and out of the homes not only of the Church-going families but also of those who do little about Church attendance and yet are none the less his to care for, then they know that he is well on the way to fulfilling the job he was put there to do.

Such steady, slogging work will entail using the unforgiving minute to the full. 'Time is elastic, almost anything can be fitted into it,' Archbishop Nathan Söderblom used to tell his clergy. If they looked sceptical, the remark was followed by another of his oft-quoted words: 'You must work yourselves to death – but slowly, please' (Bengt Sundkler, *Nathan Söderblom: His Life and Work*, p. 154).

Visiting, then, or its equivalent is of the *esse* of a priest's work. I say 'or its equivalent', because the nature of the contact of the priest with his 'flock' will be different when that flock is in a factory or a club, in a University or a holiday camp, from what it is when the 'flock' is to be found predominantly in the homes of a parish. But what matters is that the man of God should be – and should be seen to be – at the disposal of his people in the things of God, the initiative for the contact between him and them coming from *him*. It is not enough to say: 'I am here if they want me; let them come if they will.' It is of the nature of the

Good Shepherd that he leaves the comfort and security of the fold to seek for the lost. He goes to them with an eagerness born of the love of God and of man which is in him.

It is this out-going concern, this outreaching in love, which is the hall-mark of all Christian ministry, in whatever sphere that ministry be exercised. And it is this deep, even passionate concern for men for Chist's sake which should bind together those engaged in this ministry, however different their spheres of work may be. I must stress this, for there have been instances of parish clergy who have failed to understand the essentially evangelistic and pastoral work of, for example, the industrial chaplain – his work, they feel, if they do not say, is hardly the real thing! And there is the other side to the same coin; there have been chaplains in specialised spheres of work who have failed to appreciate the less dramatic and novel work, the humdrum toil, of the parish priest in his patient daily round. Such misunderstandings, tragic if they were to develop, arise from a failure to perceive that that which is common to all spheres of Christian ministry is the seeking for those who are lost – in high-rise buildings, in country cottages, on factory floors, in clubs, in hospitals, in schools, in colleges, in prisons. And those engaged in this ministry need the support of all their fellow-workers in Christ – support in worship and prayer, in study and discussion, in chapter meetings and clergy fraternals.

(iii) *He must become an expert at his craft.*

I have always hesitated to call the ordained ministry

a profession – it is so much more than just one profession among others. Yet it *is* that, in that a profession calls not only for specialised training but for keeping up to date with the thinking of others, and especially of the experts, in the field. It is a craft, and for its exercise the old tools must be sharpened and new ones called into use. A craft calls for *expertise*, and expertise can be gained and retained only by constant care.

The aids available to us are legion. I think not only of the books, at all levels of theological learning, which pour from the press (I assume that all clergy set aside annually some money for the purchase of these tools of their trade). I think of our chapter meetings. These should be much more than business meetings called for the efficient running of our ruridecanal concerns. They should be more than occasions for listening to addresses on various subjects of greater or less importance. They should be – and I hope they will increasingly become – study circles in which we help one another to grapple with some of the great truths with whose proclamation we are entrusted. They should be occasions for hard intellectual wrestling, and we should not be surprised if, on occasion, at the close of them we say to one another : 'Did not our heart burn within us while He talked with us … and while He opened to us the Scriptures?' Why should not our chapter meetings often take the form of joint sermon preparation classes, when we enrich one another so that, say in the coming Lent or Advent or Whit season, we all preach on the same theme, in our own way, but enriched by the insights of our brethren in Christ?

I think, again, of a matter of great importance as a

man seeks to become expert in his craft, but a matter for which it is very difficult to find a single word or phrase. I would put it thus. Here is a parish priest. He set out from College with high hopes and with ambitions for his ministry not unworthy of a servant of Christ. The years have passed and he finds himself in the middle of his ministry – or beyond the middle. He is reckoned, by average standards, to be pretty successful – it may be he has become a Canon, even, or perhaps a Rural Dean. He is something of a figure in the district and in the diocese. But deep inside him there is an ache, a gnawing conviction that all is not well, a kind of disillusionment with himself. It is not that he has lapsed into open sin and disgraced his cloth – not at all. In fact it is hard to define precisely why there is this inner dissatisfaction. Perhaps – who knows? – it is even a *divine* dissatisfaction, something luring him on to a greater and deeper ministry. Perhaps it is God Himself beckoning . . .?

At this point, God's man is likely to feel his loneliness. There is a loneliness which is inseparable from ministry, part of the price we pay for the privilege of exercising our ministry at all. But there is also a loneliness which God does not intend and for which He has an answer in the fellowship of His Church. Now 'fellowship' is a word which trips lightly off our tongue. Nor would I seek here fully to define it. But I would seek to tell you what I mean by it in this specific connection. I mean a friendship with another in Christ so deep that we can talk over this ache – divine or human in origin, whichever it be – and talk it over in depth. I mean a friendship deep enough to allow us to talk about our failures, hiding nothing; our own moral and spiritual failures; the poverty of our prayer; the thinness of our congregations (How many clergy are afraid to ask their brother clergy to preach for them lest they should see how few gather?); the perplexities of our preaching; the deadness of our worship; the doubts in our own minds about the validity of our faith. I doubt whether God intends us to bear these burdens alone.

'Fellowship' – perhaps that word has failed to convey the meaning which it had in New Testament days or even the idea which has been uppermost in my mind as I have spoken to you these last few moments. The word has become like an old coin and lost its original brightness. Try, then, the word 'open-ness', for this is the aspect of fellowship which I am now stressing. We must find someone with whom we can be 'open' about ourselves, our work, our motives. 'Much of our confusion comes from kidding ourselves ... The reason we kid ourselves is that we cannot stand the truth. This dwelling in unreality is one of the symptoms of emotional sickness or perhaps one of its causes ...' (I take these words from an article entitled 'Reflections of a green Bishop', by Bishop Paul Moore, Jr., in the *Bulletin of the General Theological Seminary*, New York, June 1965.)

Happy the man who has one with whom he can share such things. I care not whether he be priest or layman or laywoman, so long as he be in Christ. To share such things will be a humbling experience – a baring of the soul – an exposure of our spiritual nakedness. It will also be a revelation; for, as we venture on this course of action, we shall find that we are not alone in having this gnawing conviction that all is not well – he on whom we vent our aches and anxieties may well be in the same boat himself and thankful for one humble enough and honest enough to speak from his heart.

I realise that, in this address, I have laid myself open to the charge that I have spoken to the clergy alone and have neglected the laity in this congregation. I admit the charge – but only in part. It has often been said that a nation gets the kind of government it deserves; and I suppose that is true. It is equally true that a Church gets the clergy it deserves – after all, we have only the laity to recruit from! The point I am making is this: if the Church of England in the closing decades of the twentieth century is to get the kind of clergy it needs, it will only do so as its laymen and women see something of what the nature of that ministry is and of what it demands of its men. The tenacity of purpose which makes a man stick to his job when lesser men would flee; the steady faithfulness which is illustrated at its best by continuous visiting; the determination to become, each in his own way and according to the measure of Christ's grace given to him, an expert in his craft; these things, on all of which I have touched, demand behind the clergy a laity which realises that it is a co-partner in their ministry, though with different functions, and is therefore responsible to sustain that ministry by an understanding and a sympathy which spring from deep and continued prayer.

They might like to frame that prayer – they could hardly do better – in the words of one of the finest of seventeenth-century characters, Thomas Ken, Bishop of Bath and Wells, who thus set forth the pattern of the ideal priest:

> *Give me the Priest these graces shall possess;*
> *Of an ambassador the just address,*
> *A father's tenderness, a shepherd's care,*
> *A leader's courage, which the cross can bear,*
> *A ruler's arm, a watchman's wakeful eye,*
> *A pilot's skill, the helm in storms to ply,*
> *A fisher's patience and a lab'rer's toil,*
> *A guide's dexterity to disembroil,*
> *A prophet's inspiration from above,*
> *A teacher's knowledge, and a Saviour's love.*

However much the contemporary scene may alter, there are certain constants which remain always the same. There is the constant of the love of God revealed in Christ. There is the constant of the sin and need of man. There is the constant of the ministry of reconciliation. So long as these remain, the parson will not pass. He will still pray, and study, and visit, and preach, and minister the sacraments, and care for men as one who must give an account to God. In fact, he will continue to be a man of God and a pastor of his people. And because of that, there will be a spring to his step and a song in his heart.